PINK MOON

POEMS

PINK MOON

ROSHAN JAMES

Published by ECW Press
665 Gerrard Street East
Toronto, Ontario, Canada M4M 1Y2
416-694-3348 / info@ecwpress.com

Editor for the Press: Michael Holmes /
a misFit Book
Copyeditor: Jen Albert
Cover design: Jessica Albert
Author photo: Mathew McCarthy

MISFIT

LIBRARY AND ARCHIVES CANADA CATALOGUING
IN PUBLICATION

Title: Pink moon : poetry / Roshan James.

Names: James, Roshan, author.

Identifiers: Canadiana (print) 20230438792 |
Canadiana (ebook) 20230438822

ISBN 978-1-77041-762-5 (softcover)
ISBN 978-1-77852-233-8 (ePub)
ISBN 978-1-77852-235-2 (Kindle)
ISBN 978-1-77852-234-5 (PDF)

Classification: LCC PS8619.A645 P56 2023 |
DDC C811/.6—dc23

This book is funded in part by the Government of Canada. *Ce livre est financé en partie par le gouvernement du
Canada.* We acknowledge the support of the Canada Council for the Arts. *Nous remercions le Conseil des arts du
Canada de son soutien.* We acknowledge the funding support of the Ontario Arts Council (OAC), an agency of the
Government of Ontario. We also acknowledge the support of the Government of Ontario through the Ontario Book
Publishing Tax Credit, and through Ontario Creates.

ONTARIO ARTS COUNCIL
CONSEIL DES ARTS DE L'ONTARIO
an Ontario government agency
un organisme du gouvernement de l'Ontario

Canada Council   Conseil des arts
for the Arts   du Canada

To my children, the four who light up my world,
To my music-making man, my rock,
To the Pink Moon, which pulled ancestors from the aether,
To each reader:
My gratitude

Contents

Introduction   1

Pukka   2

Four   3

Absolution   4

Stand   5

Songs of Nature   6

42   7

Awake   8

Spirit of Her   9

Feathers and Stones   14

Pulsing   15

Saffron   16

Patrons and Possessions   17

Tree Line Sparrows   18

Traveller   19

Heartstrings and Hanging Things   20

Unfolding   21

Trans/Form   22

Striking   23

At My Grandmother's Feet   24

Edge of Time   25

Blue Skies   26

In Significance   27

Possibilities   28

Goddesses	29
Salty	30
Bind & Burn	31
Destroyer	32
Wonder	33
Treelings	34
Treetalk	35
A Song for Trees	36
Time and Place	58
Opening	59
On the Move	60
Descendent-Keepers	61
Kindred	62
Altar	63
Golden Circle	64
Mercy	65
Rebirth	66
Promises	67
That One Time . . .	68
In Our Bones	69
Moon-Ghost	70
Akashic	71
Epilogue	72
Acknowledgements	73

Introduction

Razor round with a sweet silver face
Primordial flash and roar
Of undertowing tidal commands
From a soft clamshell mouth

We can't understand who we are
Unless we understand
Sky rocks
And abyss

Why soil appears brown like our skin
The soul of trees
Birds
And all the intelligent
Animation

We are all
Connected by
Marrow and air

And to see ourselves, once in a new moon
Is to see how the cosmos roils
Behind the scenes
On the other side of the waking dream

Of skin, home, streets, and daytime activities

Pukka

I grew to be three rulers tall
sucking on tamarind candy
slurpy, complicated
at the corner of Kennedy and Ellesmere

Instinct spoke, *turmeric in everything*
Chatted up Kensington
About how it
Tasted like a travelling
Village home
A spice route cottage with a view

My mouth couldn't handle cardamom
Yet the hint of it was
The place where gods and goddesses
Emanated from jungle heat
Reuniting in the third eye

Four

Revelation is in the river of possibilities
Moulding Mongolian hills
Where something forgotten
                happened to this landscape
Before we walked on it
                a quickening of awareness
                a deep cratering of Spirit
Conquering of flesh and urgency

four horsemen
four corners of the ancient world
cradles of civilization found in four sacred valleys
four winds and directions
four agreements

how do we gauge what it means to be civilized?
what system exists that has ever found the truth?
and how does time pass on the moon?—These
are the question keys
for unlocking the matrices

speak of nurturing in terms of norming
how can we be so bold as to define what makes civility?

Absolution

I didn't know how
My mother asked for help
Because I never saw her

I held back for so long
Because of bad skin, eating disorders
I held myself small and quiet
Feeling my flaws
Chasing, coping, healing
Craving absolution

I was hiding in my own skeleton
Inside the closet of courage

Stand

I swallowed shame
In cities that never
Got my name

Took it in stride
When I couldn't take
Being a submissive wife

What else do we stand for
If not for ourselves?

Songs of Nature

Immortal
Wildly womxn-creator
Far beyond
The superficial holiness
Of idle white men
Running church as business

Recall your songs of nature
And sing for the garden's delight

Everything is more beautiful
Than we imagine it to be
With our open eyes
I want to be here
Long into the night

There is so much more of you
Of us
Where the wild things grow
Green and snow
Are the temperatures
Of deep-feeling consciousness

Pull me in and let me
Breathe
Your rain-heavy air
Fills me with potential

There is a weight to the thoughts
That come to us in the dawnlight
Light calls out to light
Across the face of benevolent dark
And the light always recognizes itself

Awake

The angel in the hall
Spoke in bell tones
Symphonies
          cascaded from its eyes
Spirit knew Their way through
My veins
Into every atom
Of awareness
And They called out
For Consciousness
To awake

Spirit of Her

She rose up from the seabed
Seaweed clinging
To her swollen head
From her hair hanging
Arms straggling
Like the kelp forests upside down
The same flowing tendrils but not the same
As her hair had been
Tightly coiled into a nape-of-the-neck knot
Under her habit, she swore her confessions
To an angry god, the god of her christened mother, and out of
spite to the older gods of origins unknown, so long-forgotten
They were symbols and numbers
Songs
Of the rising sun

Mary, may your grace find us
In the hour of our deepest need
In the jungle of our own transgressions
Mary, can you hear us
Over the explosions
Between screams and clawing metal
Mary, can you hear us at the bottom of the ocean
Beneath bodies of water
Hemmed by skirted shores

Weren't we all connected at one point
Weren't we all born from the womb
Doesn't land belong to everyone who lives on it
And the sea, the sea belongs to the blue?

But where did she come from before that
Has she been here all along?

Let the burning paper go
Who needs a label when we know warmth
In our bones, and the feel of snow

On her tongue
Are maps of wisdom
Her lands, spoken
Peace bridges built by her hands
What wars has she already paid for?

Beyond the realm
Self-recognition is a faint star
And she is an earthen vessel
A jar formed by light
She writes from the maw
Saying, it's okay to go in
Memory is the mother of mythologies

Let's rewrite the canon
With new lives and new eyes
What have we tasted of goodness
And fear
What bushes burn
When she is near
And what songs play on the radio laced with regret
Who is she now that the ghosts are gone
And what's left, what does she call forward
When the lights aren't on

They didn't know they were only catching slivers
Only some of her
Through fringed fragments of dusty glass
Her wholeness wasn't something that could be caught on camera
It would take a lifetime to know her
To learn at the feet of her joy

Feathers and Stones

I went in search of three feathers and five stones
And I tell you, truthfully
It was harder to find three feathers

Why is cold silence loud and impressive?
Why does steel make us feel safe
Yet softness draws out truth?

Pulsing

Emptiness among the stars
Hard to tell depth

Just as much as we are light-born
There is carbon and dark matter in our tangles

There are no words where we come from

Let me see you
Let me see inside life
In your veins
Inside my breath

Where the wild people sing first
Down deep into the lingering night thrall

Throat singing is the first utterance
Still pulsing through time

Saffron

Hermits line the corridors, heads bent
Saffron and gold are the mystic's robes
It is old
In these parts, within
Internal, intestinal
Systems of mystery

Patrons and Possessions

What possesses a womxn
To turn beads on a string
And what happens when the planet
Runs out of metal for the king

Do we know how to save ourselves
From ourselves
Or are we busy buying abundance

Corporate manifestos
Uphold hierarchies
It's basically the patriarchy
Coveting the Patron's trophy

What are we saying if we don't say no
To what our mothers choked on?

Tree Line Sparrows

Sing for me
Because I cannot sing as lovely
To greet the morning

Birds next door chirr trills
Talking, squawking
Listening, an easy way to slow my breathing
I don't want to disturb them from under
Cavernous green underskirts of tree folk

Quiet now
There is louder, harder sound from a distance
Bigger-beaked, wings spanning broad, nearing
Swooping faster and higher than the treeline sparrows

Traveller

Land traveller
Worlds expand at our feet
When we follow what's ours

Trees talk to us
Of standing against the storm
Wind rushes between their arms

> *We are stronger*
> *Than we know*
> *We are stronger*
> *Than we know*

We are earth and void
In our blood
Sacred chords

Birds sing to us
In the good way
Of harmony
Slowly feeling
The breeze

We awake to ourselves
When we let go

Heartstrings and Hanging Things

I have so much of myself to reclaim, to pull back in,
          loosening
Of heartstrings and left-over hanging things

Pass me the scissors
I'm about to go in

There are whole bodies hidden
In these walls
There are stories
I walled over with the loudest-looking plaster,
Cardboard and patterned paper

Of course, Time and Place started falling out
From the rafters of yesterfears

They say dark matter is the heaviness of the chaos
Held in small-seeming nuggets of cosmos

And I would argue
It can be equally as heavy
To carry the light

Unfolding

lotus heart
u n f o l d s
u n s p o o l s
gold-ribboned, layered
and laced
trembling

Trans/Form

all the good ones
come to me
to die
to destroy selves
to change form
to be transient in form

Striking

Daytime is harder for me
Night hours intrigue
At the striking of new time

At My Grandmother's Feet

Orbs and dust motes
Slow-trance suspended

Spirit found me at my grandmother's feet
Ochre carpet and afternoon heat
She circled the room
Silvering tongues of the moon

Guides: teachers, masters, loved ones, and oracles
I call them Tara of the bodhisattvas
Holy consciousness speaking with the archangels
Worship happens all around us

god is good, all the time
All the time, god is good

I am is good, all the time
All the time, I am is good

I am good
All the time
All the time
I am good

Edge of Time

Fractaling
Breathe in
And out
Consciousness
Pushes and pulls
At the edge of time

Blue Skies

I stared at her in reckless wonder
Yellow feathers fluttered
Her body quick animation
Flits and hops take her
Up and down runged branches
More chances to snag a seed or two
Sunlight matches her colouring
Her light-stepping courting
Of the blue-skyed day

In Significance

Let us give thanks for the honour
Of standing on the outer deck of a spinning chunk of dirt-
caked roots
And big saline puddles

Insignificant space-matter collected into self-declared
poignance
We are the spans of time, which have no consequence except
existence

To us
It is a beautiful arrangement of delight

Randomness making sense of itself
Mere self-recognition
            falling in and out of love
In the most natural of ways

Possibilities

It's a small stage
This spaceship
Take a bow
Little starlets
Life is in the making
Take it in and take it hot

There's enough in the well
For everyone's wishes
Throw yours in
        and hold
        your breath

When you lift your eyes
May you already see how hope
Has a way of opening
Into possibilities

Goddesses

I wish you were still here, Dolores and Amy
Let's go to rehab together
Maybe it'll be different this time
Maybe we'll linger for the last time
Come back someday, won't you
Come back to the goddesses of first light

Salty

What are the blessings and where can we find them
Let a thousand years wash over our eyes
There is medicine in memories
Buried under the roots of the family tree

Instead of flowers
Leave painted rocks at my grave
Acrylic kittens and sunrises
Anything that feels like life to the child-hearted

Rustling silver and sage
Spirit shivers up my back

Do we know how close we are?

Peace hides in plain sight
While we thirst for holy water
Through our tears

What is salty will never quench

Bind & Burn

Blood in the soil needs to be burned
Hands of the congregation
And father-founded bodies
Bound

What else is worth tossing into the pit?

Destroyer

Beautiful light bearer
Star of death

This is Shiva
The Destroyer

Sacred Mother
of Earth,
Show us the wounds
Left to pay

This is the eternal Void
Slipping the hangman's hooded sack
Over the ones it chooses to take
   for crimes too late to pay for
   loose and pathetic the hoods hang
   grey faces and sunken eyes bear the dread of being
   found out for the
unforgivable
   —betrayal of the whole

Wonder

I often wonder if stars know the names
Faded old men cast up
Claiming them
Are they okay with being followed from one end
Of Pangaea to another, bringing
Early peoples into contact with each other
I often wonder

Treelings

Emanations
Are my new friends
      we meet between treelines
      and amongst the treelings
Forest speaking, fungal networking
Beings

Treetalk

I find who I am
In their wordless chatter

My thoughts turn over
Stirring growth
At old roots

A Song for Trees

What peace do we offer trees
When we walk among them
Do they hear our tread or breath first

Do they hush
When our sighs scent the breeze

What does our peace mean to them?

Speechless to our ears
Language of shade unspoken
        dark, umbrous alchemy
In changing greens and whispering leaves
Light and breath transition
There is no idle gossip among them
Their talk: communion

Pull over the blanket of tree-speak
Closeness wraps
Around our shoulders
Where rest is found
Under thickness
Of forest sound

Winged and whistling zephyrs
Spread invisible feathers between
Piney brush-tipped skeletons
Always awake, always dancing,
Always dying while carrying life

Seedlings gambol at the feet of ancients
Where old growth breaks down to loam
And dirt erupts in slow motion

The well-planted push their own pace
Beyond the wheel of Organized Time

What dominions
Herein have privilege

Or is it more about structure and efficiency?
High towers for small beasts
Cloaked highways for small feet

Why do you grow between rocks
I can't imagine you chose it
        for yourself and your young
Was it persistent necessity?
Did one of *us* bring you here
And force you into breaking ground
You, with the dreadlocked-roots, and
        sinewed trunks more than an arm-circle around
Why do you cling to the face of rock, why if only
        to stretch out and over the riverbank
        that cuts under, exposing
Where did you learn this defiant vulnerability
Opening yourself to survival?

First enthroned as an early elder
How tall you must have been
With your regal siblings
How proper and polite
In your grace to the sylphs
Inhabitants of This Life found safety in your high walls
And you found softness in the creatures of your crown

Tear-carved face and drooping smile
Those who sit with her by the river
Where water meets
Know her heart has always been
A little bit heavy

Does the willow weep for the lost ones
Burn victims of scarce prosperity
Slumped in exquisitely carved pews
Where poor and rich sometimes try
To pray together

In congregation with the church of the forest dwellers
It is open to all
No cults of popularity
The forest knows—division introduces weakness,
It is the leading cause of corrosion in community
—and prefers to weave distinction
Into space co-created

When the sky sheds its long-frozen tears
It is reunion at your feet
It is a touch less cold and a tad more hopeful

Humidity in cupped hands
We drink shade
And cooler air
As the day sits down
It is the season of slowing
A time to savour ozone
And revel in the light serenade
Of fireflies hovering
In tall grass at dusk

Music hangs between the trees
Wherever we greet the stars

There is no judgment in the lean of an oak
The coniferous, conferring eternal gratitude
Forever points to the heavens

Folded foliage wet and wooded
Covers their chemical romance
It is a dark melting symphony
Of rot and rebirth
The rough ones with underbrush
Let it all hang out
Feverish in dreaming

we who are tawny-skinned
with ancient roots
know the importance of food and family
of holy networks and candlelit prayers
we grew up around singing bowls
tones of warmth with the scent of rich-skinned heritage
call us to imagine
wherever we are planted

arms raised in perpetual worship
how joyful to receive and transmit
wizardry through finger wands
Open Palms
pull in mothering magic
to nourish the parched crowds
proliferating on the hillside
bread and loaves multiplied for the followers

sugar sap crowns upside down
hang from the underbelly of broken branches
does the harvest hurt?
does it taste sweet
to let your blood run down?

We are from the mountains
    where the hardy survive
    where clouds time-lapse above
The sombre permanence of granite heights
Fluctuating
Under marbled skies
We feel the weather in our bones, the aether
And experience wears on our faces

Sometimes we talk about what we've seen
Sometimes we keep it close

standing near the woods
she felt like silk grass

sunlight filtering
through her skin

It was the forest that saved her
She could be alone and connected
She could be sad yet inspired
She could have many questions
And the forest would always respond

I want to be like you
Deeply rooted
Holding
Stories
And birds
And first-light

Time and Place

Hot night driving
From Paris to Newton
"Rescue" by Brilla, songstral.poetex
Clears the air
Rhythm is euphoric,
      —The Local Oracle
Of this time and place

Opening

that seed
that spark
that scrap of faith
will move
the mountains
we need moved

we will walk
as giants
in the valley

we are the opening of the land

On the Move

You are in the moon now
my spirit feels
the Spirit on the move
and all the ancestral Creators who encircle us

Mother Space holds it all

Descendent-Keepers

I take smoke from a crystal pipe
Holding the universe in its tip
We are the descendent-keepers
        of the earth and moon and stars
Within and around us

Kindred

For the moons that crossed the sky
While I spoke with my kindred self
As I pulled unread stories
To the surface of us
Of we, these ones, this rootedness

Altar

I made a sacrifice to the altar
Of a new moon
To see the ashes burn
My old transgressions
Kept under folded hands

I stepped back in time
Through myself
And woke up at nine in flannel robes

Desolation drops us to our knees
Teaches us the sacred discipline
Of letting go

but I had questions
left to answer

Golden Circle

"Draw the golden circle"
Is a call from the deep woods
We are in search of healing people

Shadows of us shimmer in darklight
Fluttering petals of heartbeats
Through film and acetate
Flicker

Mercy

Give me the ones who bleed mercy
And I will show you
Where there are open wounds
In the places they call home

Rebirth

I tasted living words for the first time
On my fire tongue
It was Spirit language
Mixed with mother's blood

And the goddesses rejoiced
In this rebirth

Who will sing the moon's song with me
   Who will sing
   Who will sing

Who will be the light in me
And who will be the dark
   I will
   I will

Promises

Promises
We whisper

To ourselves
In the dark

The Spirit keeps
With us

That One Time . . .

When the first and last
Met again
At the juncture of turning

Magnetism
And void
No light
Only matterful stuff

We are the abyss
And the expansion

One and the other
One or the other
Neither one nor the other
Both one and the other

All of a sudden
And once upon a time

In Our Bones

Spirit is in the land
In the moon
In the dark
Light and day
Are the shadows
And leave-behinds
Of god-work

Moon-Ghost

We tried to hold
The day's end up at the treetops
With our flexed-up feet
Pale to the Moon-Ghost and sunset

Who can talk about trees
Without talking about the moon
And the stars?

Akashic

Searching for home
One stone at a time
One soul at a time

Epilogue

What do you think
Her real name is?

Acknowledgements

I am a settler on Turtle Island, which is colonially known as Canada. The work I do and the land that our family lives on is part of the traditional territory of the Haudenosaunee, Anishinaabeg, and Neutral Peoples, situated on the Haldimand Tract and governed by the *Dish with One Spoon Treaty*. I am actively educating myself on First Nations' history and I am committed to advocating continuously for Indigenous rights and freedom. It is a joy to centre and celebrate the rich heritage, lasting traditions, and invaluable wisdom of the Indigenous People of Turtle Island. In doing so, we honour and call for restoration of ancient practices, with respect and care for the land and the life on it. May we continue to pursue truth and reconciliation in all aspects of community.

My deepest gratitude—First, to the land. Earth. Our Mother. Our home in this dimension. Thank you for abundance and enoughness. To the trees, thank you for sharing your stories, songs, shade, and splendour. To my family—Patrick, Ayla, Zahara, Norah, and Theodore—thank you for being my world and allowing me to be part of yours. To my spirit guides, ancestors, teachers, and loved ones—thank you for your guidance and inspiration.

Emm Gryner, you are the best coach. Working with you is a living dream. Michael Holmes, your gentle way of editing was the precise nurturing that the manuscript needed. Shannon, Jen, and the team at ECW Press—thank you for being lovely to work with.

ROSHAN JAMES (she/her) is a Tibetan-Indian multi-disciplinary artist, poet, and musician, living as a settler in southwestern Ontario. As part of the South Asian diaspora, Roshan researches and experiments to create work that embodies decolonization, identity, timelessness, mindfulness, purpose, and healing. Entrenched in her work is anti-oppression advocacy and representation of marginalized, melanated voices to help dismantle colonial, capitalistic systems. Roshan studied at Queen's University and the Centre for Medieval Studies at the University of Toronto, and she holds an Honours Bachelor of Arts degree in English Literature from York University, summa cum laude. You'll find her on social media, most active on Instagram at @roshan_james.